Where Space Bends

poems by

Anique Sara Taylor

Finishing Line Press
Georgetown, Kentucky

Where Space Bends

ACKNOWLEDGMENTS

Earlier versions of these poems have appeared in:
Adanna Literary Journal / "Mourning in Days of Joy"
Common Ground Review / "The Fragmented Path"
Cover Magazine, NYC / "Between Valhalla and Katonah"

"Writing While Driving Across the Tappan Zee Bridge" appeared on Emerge
Gallery's Blog

Publisher: Leah Maines

Editor: Christen Kincaid

Cover Art and Design: Anique Taylor
       Where Space Bends: Mixed Media Painting
       Connecticut Woods (detail): Oil Painting, back cover
       Weeds (detail): Graphite Drawing

Author Photo: Violet Snow

Printed in the USA on acid-free paper.
Order online: www.finishinglinepress.com
          also available on amazon.com

Author inquiries and mail orders:
Finishing Line Press
P. O. Box 1626
Georgetown, Kentucky 40324
U. S. A.

Table of Contents

For Penny and Nesha,
for their love and belief in me

For my wonderful teachers along the way,
for their inspiration and support

For those who continue to heal from Lyme Disease,
for their brilliant courage

Plum Island

First bought for a coat, a barrel of biscuits and 100 fishhooks,
named Manittuwond by the Pequot Nation for beach plums
that grow by its shores; its 840 acres teem with osprey, kestrels,
loons, Canada geese, gulls, ticks, white-footed mice, deer & 70
government buildings, where high-hazard pathogens are handled
through steel-windowed boxes with glove inserts for experiments.

Lab 257's germ warfare research laboratories.

Migrant birds swoop among
animals injected with virus vaccines
fed in open-air troughs. A Bio Level 3 animal
disease lab, they study tick warfare, as deer swim two
miles from Lyme to forage for food. Outside the lab, seagulls
pick at dead birds on the ground, fly between Island and mainland.

Across the Sound my parents suntan
on aluminum beach chairs. Sand burns

the bottoms of their feet. Momma hands
out salami on white bread from a wicker

basket. Low tide, I drizzle mudflat wet
sand into Gothic drip castles and moats.

I rock back on my heels, squint
at a seagull flying across the water.

        I wonder who lives there
        and what my life will be—

as another gull glides above me

low
almost stopped in the air

The Pickwick Theatre

The Undead lurch at me, flickering in black and white.
Feet propped up on railing, I cringe into the nubbed seat,
gulp down malted milk balls in Pickwick Theatre's
Saturday afternoon cave. Under domed ceiling
constellations, Greek statues shadow into wall grottos
around us. Horned fingers chase and grab at me as
I escape into Putnam Avenue's spotlight of sun.
For days the Undead stagger after me. In my hard night
bed, I stretch a rigid line of sheet up to my chin, afraid
just one toe will alert creatures under my bed—
and those that lurk in my closet.

Unaware of what real
monsters might be burrowing toxins
into my flesh, I slip into deep woods of spruce

and fir. A raven swoops
low almost touching light spheres
reflected in the lake. A spotted fawn pauses,

lifts her ears. Can she see
translucent ladies in white, dancing
the Charleston merge with tribes that once

lived here? I tiptoe down
ruined mansion stairs. A white-
tailed deer bolts through the ghost orchestra,

past remains of the formal gardens
as I curl into leaves by the black water,
the bones of my hand tucked underneath my skull

The Rosewood Bedroom

The hollow click of high heels
    drums down the oak hallway
        to the flagstone entrance, a house

of perfectly-mapped futures boxed up
    like cut flowers. Birch tree leaves
        spin millions of shades of green

in moonlight. Cricket clacks carpet
    the night heat. Does anyone know
        the names of the stars? The rosewood

bedroom by sassafras saplings and poison
    ivy vines that twist through underbrush
        down to the swamp and forest beyond,

is smaller than breath. What begins
    in the universe of a single cell till even
        bones cannot breathe. In the silence

the soul breaks, and the soul does not break.
    Past the perfect, shiny shell, the split-level
        ranch houses and crew cut lawns, planets

look as though they're floating
backward through the sky

The Bucket

Door hinges
creak open. There is
no wind, a terrible calm in
the night sky. A frigid crescent
at the bottom of a bucket. Hundreds
of polished bones that had moved within
muscle under skin. A baby mouse curled, her
mouth frozen open, pink claws outstretched. Maybe

this time
I will tell you as much as you can bear

Free Fall

A fisherman leans on the Esopus River Bridge railing
    angling for wild rainbows in deep pools, the swift
riffles and long runs trout love. Route 28 slices

into the solid wall of mountain green. A pickup truck
    brakes for sunglassed weekenders. Hair curled with heat,
visitors stroll their dogs down Main Street.

A motorcycle plows past Country Store's baskets stacked
    with tart cherries, peaches, nectar that drips down the chin.
Goggled, black leather-gloved bikers rev their Harleys

two at a time, who can tell where it begins. I drag out
    the ripped massage table, lattice 1x3's from an old
sukkah, Magic Marker a "Free" sign, prop them up

against the white picket fence for neighbors on their
    Saturday pilgrimage to the Thrift Store. Seduced by sweet
scents, barbecued chicken wings at Mama's Boy Market,

shining blue picnic tables, July heat topples us
    into a strange equation of the infinite. The promise
that this intoxicating warmth will last forever

free falls us into a version of paradise
that forgives us everything we've ever done

Silk Wall of Green

Two boys huddle in black Ford
pickup back seat, rusted-out tailgate,

gorge on raw corn on the cob. Puddled
driveway ruts glint water in the sun.

In an upstairs window a fan drones on,
I cannot find the borders in the air.

Cars race both ways past
August's silk wall of green. Words

separate into what can be used
and what is useless, as everything

trembles. I don't know what to reach for
first. A crow caws. Another answers one

note lower. Sun seeps over berries nut lush,
easy in the hand, I need to know everything.

Somewhere a phone rings as if time
had suspended us in a perfect circle

Fibrous Seeds of Milkweed

The roses almost didn't make it through
    the winter, fibrous seeds of milkweed
        and thistle. Rhododendron blossoms

candle out, large as my hand, organizing
    some invisible field. A swallow dips low,
        a sign of rain. Drinking from the well

before sunrise, we're wrapped in the skin
    of words. Up zigzagged switchbacks, we
        hike, drifting in and out of a conifer forest.

A lean-to in the clearing overgrown with wild
    ginger and garlic mustard, porcupines have
        gnawed the floor boards for salt, chipping

deep enough to unfreeze hope. If the wind
    blows toward you, a bear may not smell you
        until he is too near. Light drains, turning

spring trees into black silhouettes—or
    an invitation for magic. If the reluctant
        ground shifts beneath you, do not run.

Back away slowly. From here
    if Earth falls away (undulating cracks
        of dark water below) you can see across

the valley into the lining of each
    moment, a truth I cannot explain.
        Even with a voice so little, can you feel

a melody that sews together
    the edges? Blesses every thing that is
        upside down, has layers, opens up—

the unmendable beauty of what is speckled,
has clawed feet or makes us weep

Taco Tuesday

My Celica grinds over parking lot
craters behind Main St. I carry Nesha in her
red plaid bag up Sportsman's ramp. Taco Tuesday.
Chicken, beef, bean or fish. $1 a taco. $3 for a Margarita.

Vicky's been nailing roofs, Chip
installing insulation. Julie dashes out
in search of a lost owl. Patricia & Amy
weave around to Diana Mae's table after
Chorus. Nesha barks when I hustle her down
the ramp. Sixteen years old, still scampering under
the oaks (three barefoot girls patter after us to watch).
Crickets croak like ducks, clatter & quake in the August
evening, waiters surf tables, sling margarita & taco stacked
trays. Nesha scarfs down two chicken and one fish leaving me
three lettuce tacos as JoAnne & Jerry run in with Julie and The Story:

> A biologist had spotted a wounded owl. They traced deep forest
> meridians praying markers would hold. The broken branched
> pine tree six paces past a second hill, after a boulder in the river
> bend. An echo, a nod from the Great Owl God. They found him,
> broken winged, trembling in the dusk. Wrapped him in towels,
> eased him into the carrier.

> Afraid of missing the raptor wildlife rehabilitator at Winchell's
> Corners, they gulp down bean tacos and rush out. The exquisite
> tumult of voices over a beach of clinking plates, what holds the
> skin of our lives together here.

Down the ramp (hiding my own broken wing),
in the car, Janice Joplin belts out
> *Freedom's just another word for nothing left to lose*

as I'm thrown back to a time
when I was helpless in the dark unable
to fly. In the driveway, I look up at the three
mountains that hold us suspended in their palm—

wondering how we get lost
and how we are saved

as the Victorian roof peak
framed perfectly
slices open the night sky

Fierce Moon

The fierce moon twists shallow dreams, waking me
into the whisper of roots and wild berries whose canes
stretch through overgrown meadows into marshes

and unruly fields. I wander tangled creek side
along rotted railroad ties. Dim light wraps skeletons,
decayed trains in rain-soaked sheets, the bitter

taste of spring grass. A dragonfly biplane dive-
bombs my head, rattling his noisy cargo. By
abandoned railroad tracks before dawn, thorned

dewberries scratch my ankles, tear at my jeans,
their barbs that protect sweet fruit from wild turkeys
and bear cubs. I gather elderberries to ferment,

apples for wine. I set blueberries beside your screen
door before rain peels apart the clouds, cross-hatching
reflections of fallen leaves into mud puddles. A summer

riot of church bells vibrates the street, awakening
the memory of musty bibles with family names, lemon
oil on dusty pews, starched Sunday best. The precious

and profound entangled with wounds of the unforgiven.
We haunt a shy weave of street shadows, trying
to trust this house, this garden and every thing under

the fierce moon, wanting only to believe again

Hooked Claws of Wild Roses

Hooked claws of wild roses
grab at my skirt, twist layers of fabric
into bunches around my ankles. They scrape

my skin as if they knew me.
Ruthless, I hack at dead branches, fling them
into the wheelbarrow and shove them onto the burn pile.

Gunmetal sky, dark matter begins
to form in elongated wisps. With a mirror
I trace the geography of my body, from luminous

edges to hidden notches and misty
valleys where ticks like to hide. This morning,
two murderers hacksawed their way out of Dannemora's

honor block through steam pipes, a system
of catwalks. They tunneled into a June morning
awakening the fugitive in me beyond the vanishing point.

The useless haunts of empty hands
and invisible prisons, I drink from the well
before sunrise. Our thirsty beaks long for rain.

Even on a perfect day,
unasked questions circle the world
we so believe in, unsure how we'll break free—

or who will walk away

Mayflies

Forsythia unfolds among wildflowers before
    ailanthus can close in and cut off the sun. From edges
    of the marsh, the call of spring peepers reverberates.

After warm rains begin and migrating warblers return,
    females lay eggs. Hundreds. Without hearing or sight,
    newborn raccoons show only a shadow of mask on pale

fur. Training cubs to search garbage for apple cores, lasagna
    scrapings, watermelon rinds, mother bears lumber down
    from caves in the hills behind our houses before dawn.

Cluttered sheets of daily to-do lists, we try so hard to hold
    everything together. I dump perfume bottles, torn boots,
    empty shaving cream cans into garbage bags, sweep

up piles of grime-coated coins. A roommate who left in the night.
    Even fan blasting on high cannot eradicate the sickening reek
    of vanilla. Against this emptiness, mouths without any working

parts, some mayflies live for only an hour, their one purpose
    to reproduce. We hack through a tangle of days in search
    of meaning, our rapid wingbeats—as mayflies swarm up

from undulating currents of deep water, inking out the sky

The Harvest

With thick leather gloves, I pry open razor spiked
hulls. Litters of backyard treasures into a card-
board box. Mahogany chestnuts, their translucent

membranes wrap brain-grooved flesh that
splits apart after roasting. When. On my arm,
something—a strange scab attached deep.

Under jeweler's loupe. A deer tick. Engorged.
Her blood meal interrupted before she can
overwinter in leaf litter, her forest-floor nursery

for eggs, thousands that cluster following
an invisible plan. A teeming mound forms. Red.
The outer bite. The innermost circle pulses blue.

A crater. Stealth pathogens drill into nerve, joints,
spin through rivers of blood and lymph to far off
lands of distant skin. They dive into cells, alter

form. I zip the tick into a plastic bag. Stuff jeans
and turtleneck into the dryer. Broken as the husks,
I rush to the shower to scrub with rose soap,

as the water all around me turns into tears

Between Valhalla and Katonah

On the Harlem line to Katonah eating chicken
wings and oat bran bread, out my window, rock

strewn stream winds through high stone. Luminous
clouds, dark blue to translucent pearl, promise glory

or storm. Alemony my pink-spotted-butterscotch-
amoeba-faced-gray-and-white-striped cat, about to

die. Valhalla. Maples on yellow hill, green and brown
suburban landscape autumn reminds me life is not

this page. All hell breaking loose, alive and hungry
as she dies. Your soft cheek, her tumors, silver train,

moving reflections, and who will listen to who as
all the squared-up-picket-fenced green-lawned yards

sit calmly bicycle strewn

The Spirochete

Begins a rushing sweet enough to blow apart
the limb bone of an angel. Red waved, rocket
your dark ocean—soar, sail your nurture glow.

O sweet organs, light units—our swoop, spin, circle
glorious spiral spectrum, refract hallowed prisms.
This rise, rotate, glide, of viscous fluids, luscious.

Heaven bath! Filament twist! The pierce of cuticle,
the inner membrane, bathe the warm deep. Delicious
mucous! O give thanks to you, Bounteous Tissue

Host, even The Gods tremble at your beauty. Joy
enough to split apart the soul. We tunnel the under
sea of your cells, burrow descent into (and curl)

even for eternity where no one can find us. We wait
for the re-awakening. The Worshipped Tick
to inject new sleepers, to resuscitate our glory

The Raspy Call of a Barn Owl

Knees shoulder width apart, ankles flexed,
I dig up tender dahlia bulbs, pull them out

before the first frost. Wrapped in plastic
bags, buried in sawdust filled boxes, I shove

them onto basement shelves, small bones
of the dead. Tremper Mountain black

against afternoon sky, I gather scattered
apples and pears into baskets, hunt for

clues in the pale wingbeat, the raspy call
of a barn owl. A chickadee cracks open

a sunflower seed shell, chips out bits
discarding the husk. The sadness of first

maple reds, across the road, a neighbor
the color of branches walks out of the frame,

like someone from long ago. I pinch off
shriveled fruits encouraging the ripening

of large tomatoes. Snipped savory and sage
dry upside down from beamed kitchen

ceiling beside lavender and dill, as the equinox's
perfect balance of light and dark approaches—

as I wait, hungry in the night

Between Wild Angels and the Fiery Forest

Between wild angels and the fiery forest,
children canter across the playground at dusk.

Endless rows of yellow buses shimmer the late
day heat. Suddenly no birds. No wind. Circles melt

into each other, elongate across the windshield.
(Breathe threadlike through filaments to catch

enough air.) The white sky whispers before it
begins. One step. A network of invisible cords.

Then it's gone. I float above the surface, try
to remember I am not the vanishing point, but

dune grass sends roots downward to anchor
windblown sands, and willow thickets grip

soggy meadow sediment, opening this silver
morning as every atom connects with every other.

Even shade-soaked impatiens unhook their double
wings as if only they could bring alive their dead

Gravitational Pull of the Hidden

I wake into the balance point between two
wings, sun-wet greens early, the intoxication

of garlic mustard. A ring-billed gull soars low
over the park. Tree shadows ink their lines. I hike

the pebbled path past breakwater to inlets as
if I could depend on clouds that crumble near

the horizon. Not only the hollow bones that began
with finger tips before birth, the initial imprints

released into blood. Ducks in moon-backed sky
ballet, their v-shaped flight, have long ago braved

storm winds for kinder weather, how will they find
their way. Scientists count flocks that circle Earth

before sunrise, silhouettes attached to the burning
cord that follow invisible cues. They fly the lonely

disc as if they believed their wings could save
them. A late migrant, I trace my circuitous route,

the invisible map, the edges of an empty room.
I draw an imaginary line between two fading stars

Again

I turn away from the window.
Red and yellow, maples cross-hatch
the sky with autumn chill.
I burrow under the patchwork quilt.

Focus. Each. Cell. Stop
the shattering, this eggshell skull.

Somebody props me up,
spoons honeyed yogurt
between paper lips.
My ribs, raw blue pain.

Wind wrestles
the dead catalpa leaves.
A cardinal flits away.

A haze around the hands
as they were
before the light left them—

Who will I pray to now

This Distance from the Moon

Begin with your failed concept of grace,
    how first leaves drop their blood, how death
weaves her voice through it all. Measure

the names. Those who have gone before us,
    a diameter of hope divided by this distance from
the Moon. A spider web glows in first-morning light,

the sum of an unfinished life. Wild rabbits
    drop part-chewed pears behind the green fence.
Half alone, I weave a cocoon of my hair, blood-

root mixed with bitter melon seed, the house
    of skin we wear. November maples toss the sky
haywire, having spun their whirligigs furiously into

the drop zone. Even wrapped in chemicalled
    air, Earth continues her circles. A candle,
a feather, a wooden spoon, what have we done?

The ground is littered with angels.
Pray for a mad storm to sweep through

Unmapped Sky

Our wind-whipped jackets,
we hiked the pebbled beach by
breakwater, past inlets behind your house,

leaned into slicing cold.
You cut purple statice, arranged
them in a cobalt vase in front of the mirror.

Strawberries set in crystal
dishes, homemade banana bread
with sweet butter. We settled cross-legged

on white floor, sipping
black tea. Now a row of oblong
windows separates clouds into banks

of threes, your measured
breath. Six of us hold hands
around your bed. White sheets

tucked under your shriveled
wings, blankets folded as if neatness
could hide you from death. Brittle bones

of bivalve dusk, what
do you see as you drift away
from us? In parking lot night, my circular

spinning etches neon pinpoints
into the vast black, streaking wild arcs.
Now who will save me from the unmapped sky,

this immense heaven

Clawed Rains Hollow Out the Sweet Air

Clawed rains hollow out the sweet air.
Sealed in by windows, each day allots us

three minutes less light. Wishbone chest,
transparent skin draped over bird bones,

your shoulders shudder forward in pain.
Blood supply inadequate to keep tissue

viable, a nurse dabs cream on cracked
lips. Blueberry veins, your glazed eyes

sink in. There is no further option for cure,
I listen through my skin. I perch by your cage

of branches, life suspended by a thread
from a feather. I call on the perfect white

sheets, on the orchid beside your bed,
dried leaf of body. I call on the last moment

I am alone with you. I call on the one who
has not yet saved me and any other god

who could love her sleepless creatures—
that you float above the surface. Let go

of the vanishing point. What can you
see from there? What will you risk

for the unknown

Silver Spotted Leaves Flip Wildly on Hinges

Each in her own way gets ready for work.
One rushes to grab papers and cell phone,
another slices peaches into yogurt. I unlock
the back door. Step out. Pause below
the Woodstock Chimes I gave you.
       I stand under them, you said *and let*
       the sound vibrate my whole body.
Sun in dogwood and Japanese maples, the veil
between worlds grows thin. Moired patterns
of October light in ailanthus, what did you dream
as you drifted away? Small bones of the dead,
fainter than new-born stars invisible to the eye,
I try to understand simultaneous shadows,
the layers of the known and the unknown. Was it
the Solar System that circled low, the last moment
I was alone with you? Did particles colliding near
the horizon keep the night sky from ever becoming
totally dark? Silver spotted leaves flip wildly to green
as every island, every mountain is moved out of place.
Naked without my shawl of words, I spin around.
I look down the back trees to the pond below.
I call for you

Who Will Cross the Sea

Earth spin turns Jupiter into strings of light
that slash the sky, streaking the ancient wrinkled

map. Stars grow invisible emptying out the breaking
shadow. 4 a.m. I'm consumed with infrastructure.

The standard deviation of bone density below
the mean, the crooked tooth in front that defines

my character. Face mites crawl out of hair
follicles in darkness to mate. The illusions we

live in tangle through crawling vines and daily
plans. Icicles in sharp edge of night dangle

from steep pitched roofs. I search in silence,
exempt from love of any kind, while skeletons

love for so long. Outside the cave on terraced
slopes, outlined leaves shadow their faces. Did

a vague compass light their way? Their skulls
gaze at each other wanting so much. These six

thousand years they've lain together sun-split,
knees curled to chin as if they'd crossed the last sea

Wall of Fire

Naked trees hatch inked lines
    into the magenta sky. They crack
    and sway like branches of my family.

Over flatland reed and swamp, we sped down
    Harlem River Drive, past viaducts, steel
    bowstring arch of Hell's Gate Bridge,

and concrete block projects into tunneled
    stations. The rattle of storm windows in wind.
    A pigeon lands on the railing, black eye

ringed iridescent inside the equation.
    The day after you died, a spacecraft flew
    past Neptune's largest moon. I cross out

your false name and pencil your true name
    into the plain wooden casket. Silent
    behind the curtain, I witness your long box

rolling into the wall of fire, blankets folded
    as if neatness could argue with a death
    that swallows all light from background

stars, forever entangling the braid of the living
    with the dead. I hold my hand up to the sun
    to see through to my bones, as pilgrims walk

sunwise round holy wells—
praying for what has already been lost

Taste of Snow on Your Wrist

The distance to the center is longest
in the morning. A membrane, a sour ancient

trick of the clock. More than time,
something in the cells. How a frame

holds together, even if you cannot understand
how mist connects with the mesh of it.

Not just the thought, the taste of snow
on your wrist. The sound of the mountain

disappearing just as it seemed
you could touch—or it could help you

find what you most needed

Mourning in the Days of Joy

The Last Day of Sukkot

On the final day of Judgment as the New Year
    is set, I tighten my quilt, a shroud around me.
I sink into the tired couch, as far away families

celebrate in breakable houses of two-and-a half
    walls. Fronds to see through to stars, who pray
with the spine of palm, two mouths of willow,

three eyes of myrtle, a heart of citron. They dip
    bread in honey. I pour green tea from a thrift
store carafe. They circle seven times, carrying

bundles. Five. Willows to strike the ground five
    times, shake loose the leaves. As it is decided
who will be judged, how we are loved and whether

the rain will fall. Dark matter begins to form as
    the vanishing point of my life shrinks like a dying
star, the fragility of humans. Surprised the world

continues to turn, I break the commandment of joy.
I close my eyes to hide my sin of weeping

Earth Tilts Toward Its Little Star

Night has either passed or has not come yet.
    Homesick for something beyond what I can see, I
search the strange city for you. Stars blank as ghosts,

do you blame the restless uncertainty of humans,
    the paper cut-outs of our lives? The Moon pulls away
from Earth, a mirage of inner direction. An icy comet

brightened to the first magnitude and sped into the Sun
    the day you died as ashes fell all around. Crickets shake
low to the ground, a haunting that never leaves.

A hole in the tall grass leads into the earth. I want to
    fall into it like wild rabbits do. Disappear. Like some
things do. Like you. If I could unlock the names

of all the things I may never know. A train arrives
    illuminating the station like angels' wings. It begins to rain.
Still I wait for you. Do you weep without knowing why

Prayers like Summer Honey

Hours singe and crackle around the bed.
Losing faith in the horizon, robins hide
from the wind. The world stopped
in this narrow coffin of night, I pray

for sleep to pull me under. Wind rattles
curled rhododendron leaves against the bay

window. Ghosts mumble so loud, my dream
voices unravel. I gather pronouns and lost
loves, wait for the moon to grow dark again.
Do I admit this loneliness belongs to me.

Wanting so many things, I crochet another
row to widen the circumference, the garden

room rug crafted from thrift store yarn. I
stitch until my hands cannot open anymore.
This does not release me from the white
noise of now. I bang against the locked door

of happiness, its secret safe from me. I will
my hinged heart to creak open. Rubble from

generations spills across the soft skin of earth.
I search for a prayer that could split apart two
halves of the universe to sing through me like
summer honey. For god to send angels—

battalions to hammer out an answer,
deliver flocks of wild birds to swoop down

with a key to their forbidden language

Curving Limb of Earth

Measured lengths of tired lace by tenement
walls filter in only the required allotment
of light. Circular iron-wrought railings

shift shadows on black slate landings. Each
particle drifts with its own momentum
through the void, a beautiful fire hovering

within. Even with the promise at birth
of ovaries—two hundred thousand eggs
in their pocket of time, only four hundred

will ever bloom. Atriums of the heart having
taken shape, a host of children's voices echo
from the playground below. Shock waves

from a dying star scatter clouds of diamond
dust into distant articles of time. We sleep
alone so many years. Blind to the dream

of a solid world, night and day in fragile
balance, manageable equations dissolve
at the edge. A hunger that never leaves.

To conceal my short wing, I hug
the curving limb of Earth,
follow purple footsteps in the night

Paper Dreams

An asylum woman. I draw her curled fetal,
sweat-soaked hair. Angels falling all around her.

I hold on for one second. Then one second more.
This illness. It is all I am, nerves of scraped glass.
I pass out. I wake. I don't know who I am.
They tell me I cannot have a baby.

I am quiet. I understand.
I am patient. I live beside life.
I cannot have what other people have.

Another fever. My breasts swell.
It hurts to move.
         They ache when the wind blows? the doctor asks.

My cells pretend to come alive.
     In the dream we spin in a meadow—
     No—a tropical island. And we're swimming.

In the book you're a reptile creature smaller than a kidney bean,
webbed fingers, eyes half-lidded. Eight weeks. Is your tail dissolving,
Little Bean? Fast beating heart, are you perfectly formed?

     In the dream I chase you.
     You grab balloons in chubby fingers, running across
     the lawn. You turn back laughing, your jam-smeared face.

I want to keep you. More than anything,
Little Bean. I keep you secret.

I draw fetuses curled in the womb—floating
in shadow. Turned. Breech. Pulled with forceps.
Or perfectly-formed newborns. Nursing. Blissful.

As the poison seeps into our cells. As this illness encloses us.
I make believe I can keep you. But you already know—
the dead don't give birth to the living

Stoneswept

Gas-laced dust particles batter winds
from a newborn star. Each with our own

momentum, we drift through the void.
It was cold and there was only a slight drizzle

the day I was born. I try to accommodate
uncertainty, the twirl of the falling maple seed.

I skate the pencil outline of a pond, before wind
spins me into space. Individual parts of the shadow

circle an anarchy dance. They whisper they are
not real, but why would they tell us anything

else? A driveway puddle's reflection of leaves
glitters, unspooling the sun. Afraid of toppling

this daydream's orbit, I try to anchor
the outer tissues. The hollow organs. I press

my body length against the wood floor, push
the skin of my cheek into the cotton weave

of cabbage roses. I breathe into the place where
the core splits. A door slams. Then silence.

The phone rings again. This time they leave
a message. I draw the shades all the way down.

Whatever it was, it is gone now

Elephants, Spirochetes and the Moons of Saturn

I pour colored buttons into a bowl, fold off-season
    dresses into flowered piles, load discarded blank-backed
junk mail onto the daily to-do clip board. Without

a compensating balance wheel, some days it's all I can
    do. Life suspends itself, an icicle from a sharp pitched roof,
a gnawing inside every morning. Half woman, half bird,

I sign a petition for elephants chained to concrete floors
    in rusty, barren zoo barns, alone through the winter night.
Spirochetes flare with the new moon. I stare at wing-shaped

clouds, then a spot on the ceiling where plaster
    is crumbling as if only this in life mattered. Placid
lakes of Saturn's moons reflect the Sun, mirror like.

Thoughts of running away fill the starless sky,
    spinning out in ringed layers. Something raw forming
I can hardly see, I try to trust as Earth falls away

How to Carry a Chicken Home

Some say this is possible if you do not look up
at forty stories of chrome window sprockets reflecting sun.

I carry two pounds of pink breast and thigh sinews.
Flesh slabs tucked into Styrofoam, shrouded in plastic.

So heavy no one in the world could ever carry them. Ignore
the flutter of navy blue suits that swarm from office to lunch.

Ignore the ocean of sky so wide you cannot see where it begins,
your bones embedded in cement, the failed seed at the center.

Meditate on juices, bubbling as if savory
 mouthfuls could erase all memory.

Let the mirage of shimmering couch
carry you forward as you whisper this mantra:

> *One.   More.   Block.*
> *One.   Block.   More.   Home.*

Soon you may even be able to lift one foot.
Don't ever admit—

> *You   may   not   be   able   to   do   this*

Ghostly Cocoon

Snow dismantles the day piece by piece,
spinning a ghostly cocoon the color of egg
shell and cornsilk, bleached bones and ivory

gulls. Droplets freeze into white lace, melt
then harden again among drifts and mud.
I throw my list into the fire. A forbidden

deviation from religious law, farthest on
the spectrum from violet, some countries
ban all that is red today, a stain of danger.

They crushed into dye the red from bodies
of female insects that lived long ago in roots
of certain herbs. Some send a Valentine key

to unlock the giver's heart. A cardinal,
feathers the color of match tips and blood,
pomegranate and fire, perches in a nearby

holly bush shattering the invisible grid.
Snow again tonight. Translucent crystals
topple out of a hole in the sky. Hope stretched

so far it's barely a hair wide. Frozen under
ground, daffodils hesitate. Small in the road
and unsure which part I'm supposed to play,

I run, but I cannot find you

Which Frequency God Remembers

Dreamless, I sleep as spiders
    stitch together the universe, unsure
        which frequency god remembers.

Another mouse seduced
    by a handful of sunflower seeds
        did not make it through the night.

With gloved hand I fling
    her rigid body into shriveled
        rhododendron leaves that crowd

against Victorian windows to hide
    me from the world. A short prayer to
        the god of house mice, sacred bodies

inside kitchen walls.
    I crouch by the door
        in new fallen snow—

        Forgive me, my bitter little sins,
        the marbling of unmended mind.

Branches knot their icicles,
    unwilling to let go. On days
        I count the deaths, February

has no answer. I tone a jagged
    throat sound, red with desire or
        regret—which rips apart the soft

fall of everything pure
    from cloudless sky, where
        outer edges shine like eggshell.

It's all I can see from here

Blizzard's Breath

The soft fall of everything pure from cloudless sky,
    there is no imprint of life. An attempt to reach
    the street, I shovel, hoist, drop onto powdered
    mounds piled high by the driveway. I lean on

my shovel. Turn back to the Victorian layered
    in crystal blankets, that has patiently waited
    through Februaries these one hundred years.
    Her straight angles passed from stranger

to stranger through generations of documents,
    though some have loved her. I search snow
    drifts for old legends. Did we dream enough
    here? Temperatures near zero, we do not feel

her complain. Cold blasts lash rhododendron's
    tight-fisted curls against the bay window
    that hides me from the world. No birds
    in the terrible blank page of bloodless sky.

Bone bark of trees, wind-bleached powder
    storms my gray silhouette hollow inside.
    Blizzard's breath turns memory blank,
    dissolving all of my questions. When—

shadowy, a doe steps out, eye level

Earth's Broken Rib

Electric courtroom drama reruns flash my laptop
blue, weave in and out of dreams. Two degrees

below zero, two hours before dawn. Shadows
flutter, swallow light from background stars.

February's steep hill has far exceeded her limit of
below zero days. This experiment of nerves and flesh,

the frayed sash. Cardinals and sparrows build their
nests in rotten snags, decomposing branches of birch

in search of a vanishing point they can believe in.
The fragility of humans. Survivors' pinched bodies

curl in boxes, hands sealed with cold. Inside
a cocoon of sky, decades mirror each other

somewhere beyond what I can see. My small socked
feet trace the pattern of the rectangular rug's border.

I circle the living room's circumference, pray
for a god who could love her sleepless creatures

The Sauna

Naked on wood slats, locker keys scorch a spot
    on my wrist, the hiss of steam on stone.
My juices bead down shoulders and shins.

New Guinea Tribesmen believe sweat the essence
    of spiritual power. To stop evil spirits from
stealing even a drop of precious fluid, they

thrust their spears into dirt before leaving camp.
    Knees roasting, a fire at the center, minions
of microbes bob in sweaty seas. My heart presses

into rib bones hot enough to boil fear out of my
    hide. Elbow hiding my eyes, I wrap myself
in a sweltering shroud and weep where no one

can save me. Spirits who live in the rock, let
    this fever awaken white blood cells, purge
this body of toxic demons who lurk in my flesh.

Here, where Finns birth their babies and Russian
mourners warm the living souls of their dead

Twenty-Two Days

I pay attention to details.
When the snow melts,

I gather stones,
lie down by the stream

next to your bones.
Twenty-two days mark

the first year without you.
Fruits have fallen in the orchard.

I turn toward the wall
in my sleep.

Alone in a clean house, small
inside a locked-down wheel

I collect full moons
(this one half gone).

I search the boundaries of the Sun
for a trace, a similar god,

a hint of where you are—
if you are

link

The broom splits gossamer blankets apart,
snow crystals flutter into the air, dispersing
what could save me or what could pull me
under. If I could glide the first hard-shelled

minutes, my four-chambered breath, cawed
wings before morning. Inked lines of winter
tree shadows bend into the hill as if they could
make it matter, I can no longer remember

the words. Thoughts circle, anxious, as if
I could cancel their ability to fly. The clock's
second hand freezes forever on this moment,
the silence of an open vessel. A call returned

two minutes too late, an accidentally erased
phone message. I marvel at creatures who
sleep in flight. I blow dust from a skull as
my mountain blood thickens. Here is my list:

Tonight temperatures will sink into single
digits. The whole world is blue. In my room,

eyelids like a bird, I do not blink

To Wormwood

Wise women and midwives crush your leaves,
  a witch's blessing to unleash the acrid oils,
    magic lessons passed down between burnings,
your jagged leaf stalks winged at the margin.

Aromatic shrubs from rocky slopes or barren land,
  they burn your powders with sandalwood in grave-
    yards at midnight to call up spirits of the dead,
the risk of absinthe, the intoxication of vermouth.

Dancers twine your silky fibers into garlands
  chanting prayers to the Goddess of Salt. But you
    do not fool me, your filaments that mimic
the pathogens' killing spin. Bacteria that spews

into mucous membranes. I know the sorrow
  of your nature, your acrid terpenoids that spiral
    into a solar system of cells to block the microbes'
razor churn. So caustic, so volatile you force

infants to wean, you do not scare me. Your
  venomous essence is not as sharp as my
    shattered soul. I dissolve each drop into
clear water, breathe into the lining of this moment.

Let this wash me, let this poison me, let this
  penetrate the hide of the spirochetes and scatter
    their swimming minions. Let this gather up
all the parts of me I gave away to bargain for life.

Please.
Whisper your bitter secrets to me

Hatch

Mist on the mountain erases inked lines
of winter trees. I search for an outline,

something sturdy, the imprint of a stalk.
Ordinary matters in a complex system,

sirens whir to a pitch then fade. Translucent
drifts, a flurry of hexagonal ice crystals

hide what used to be true. I try to believe in
the smallest things, even if no one is listening.

My wings too short and round to fly, I twist
the membrane of words around my shoulders.

If I could unstitch the edges of skin, find
the opening that would tear apart everything

that's come before. Like those who cling
in wet clumps. Naked, their eyes closed, they

crack the dome of the universe open, scattering
trails of crumpled shell in search of a beginning

The Longest Month of March

Bone broth simmers on the stove. I consider
the harshest month of March. Hesitant, snow
drifts down the color of vanilla blossoms
and onions, potato flesh and dandelion seeds.

A nest of slender fibers, is this how it was
meant to be. The UPS man in plain brown
drops a package on the back porch. A chickadee
clings to the winter-withered rhododendron,

harps on two notes. Her chick-a-dee-dee-dee
warning intensifies. Under the frost line
ants tunnel and cluster deep into concealed
nests, even the sterile wingless females.

Anchored in shadows of children not born,
hours dissolve. Iron wheels of a dream,
in the distance, a murmur of something
not audible. Earthworms chew their way

through soil, secreting forward. Their fluid
filled chambers that pass for bone, can you
hear them breathe through their skin? I pay
attention to details, fold yesterday's laundry,

measure the exposed roots of the empty
room. I blend into a dawn that dissolves
my song. Sometimes you come back to me.
Did I think I would understand the language

Oreos, Eggshells & Jello

The bleached sky swallows the North Star
    taking even the mountains with it.
I search computer catalogs for inspiration,

ways to slip through, as if color could save
    me. There are seed packets. Baskets of beans
and cucumbers. Beets and mustard greens.

I read: Dust-covered house plants cannot breathe.
    I pluck withered leaves from the angel wing
begonia. Tattered tee-shirt, warm water damp,

I smooth the leaf, base to tip, as if I could feel it
    inhale. There are egg shells into plant starters,
milk jugs into greenhouses. There are checkerboard

cakes, drizzled with cross-hatched chocolate,
    vodka-soaked Jello shots, gutted Oreos restuffed
with Kahlua-infused pudding into drunken Oreos.

I lift my rose hips tea glass to the day's first light
    as if all my past lovers didn't live a faraway
life with a new love. I twirl to bell-like sounds

that spin the dark room around me, cling
    to a pale pink promise that this winter can
finally end and flowers will try to begin again.

I whirl until the line that separates
    everything that belongs to heaven
from everything that belongs to earth,

disappears—and the rising sun
    empties the sky of each star
and all the things I wanted to ask you

Bittersweet's Slender Nets

Snow needles erase disintegrating trains,
breaking open a secret sound. Intermingling
lines of winter branches clack their frozen

naked against magenta skies. I try to outwalk
the circumference, a membrane that separates
me from where it begins. Bittersweet straggles

slender nets, twining through torn fences and
battered hedges like those who haunt me still.
Glittering smiles locked in black & white, their

cigarette smoke circles a fragile, restless empire.
Those who can no longer apologize paint
an opaque film over truth, confusing my own

damaged geography. Eye patch Scotch-taped
together, my fingers shadow the glass. I spread
my hands across sun-striped clouds to measure

this distance to heaven. Slide down a steep
embankment of leaves and mud to the street,
where the road is widest at my feet

The Spirochetes' Last Metamorphosis

The shimmering promise,
the acid sugar of hollow ponds.
In the beginning, our axial filaments,
we spewed bacteria, the spread of clouds,
circled, soared, sailed the baths of your flesh.
Delicious mucous. Fragrant, a canopy forest of tissue,
our spirals, Gracious God, leapt to glorious light reflections.

Now your viscous ponds wrinkle. Membranes crack dry, the starve
of your terrible oxygen-pumped chambers. Your wicked herbs,
invisible magnets that weigh us down, O suffocation! Our sad
songs thread faint. No longer able to swim, can you hear
us, God Host? Will you answer our cry for honey,
our crave of rain? Uncertain of our next breath,
we call you. We fall between interlaced
shadows that flicker transparencies
like rain. Our fragile ribbons
unravel. Why do you
forsake us

Yesterday's Words Toppling into a Strange Room

I wake into yesterday's words
toppling into a strange room.
Skeletons of frozen trees,

a slow climb through morning.
By the empty feeder a winter
bird in the leaves unmarked

meshes somehow, even when
mist is low in the mountains.
I don't know how there is light,

the story moves through rain,
why some fly, flow over rocks,
break their shells into life,

sing like it mattered or trust
what comes as if it were easy.
But isn't this where time stops?

Isn't this where
you're closest to the truth

What Varies from the Mean

Ice crystals plowed
into corduroy rows stack
into stone-cluttered heaps. The town

plow scrapes frosted piles
that block the driveway in again.
Hours sink and fall between whirling white

flakes. Haven't we exceeded
the limit of dark days? No warmth
in sight, I carry grocery bags in through

March's starched
monochrome. Lentil soup
warms on the stove. Sunflowers

crisp in the oven. For days
bone broth simmers. Minerals to
restore the necessary mass that varies

from the mean. Like witches,
crones boil bones down into soup
to wake up cells, improve the density

of solar systems turned
ghostly. When we can no longer
see the road ahead, when snow fools us

with its beauty,
and even the gods
have forgotten us. When

we don't know what
we'll have to let go, it begins
to disappear. Whatever it was we thought

we'd wanted so much

Bird in the Cardboard Box

The bird of my cardboard chest is ripping
the shutters off. Face of metal, hands
of stone, shake the months that hang like

falling crystals. Earth's delicate surface
too close to the Sun, in the absence
of a compensating balance wheel, I call

on the quarter moon. I lace up Gore-Tex
membraned running shoes, spiked
traction pins to grip mirrors of ice. Head

phones adjusted, thumb pad gloves to
touch screen, I pull windproof breathing
shell overhead, snap on reflector wrist

bands. Lift, pace, stride the center of gravity.
Sweat freezes the smooth shell of my
forehead. Bowed full throttle into wind,

I race the dark. Stars trail above the horizon
turning everything into possibility. I sprint
past red tail lights, gull feathers taped

to my shoulders
as if I could fly

Into the Wild Arc

The clatter of glasses,
the clink of knives and forks weaves
through the main dining room's conversations.
I wander past leather lounge chairs by the stone fireplace

where a woman is playing
"Für Elise" on the grand piano. Arpeggios
stumble, halt the first section's tempo. Ungainly
fingers repeat the fractured theme, unable to enter into

the resolution we all need.
I pound apart textured glass doors,
opening into first-morning trees, etched
straight up in honest lines where the beginning is.

Mountains black against white
sky, mist slides across the surface. A dog
barks. Are the clouds moving, or is it the Earth?
A car pulls into traffic. Cold gives way to sun. Five

cardinals perch, dark spots
in branches, contrasting the snow.
A handful swoop down to join them. Eight... twelve...
dozens... In sudden beat the flock darts up into a wild arc

unafraid of the void

Taproot

Fierce rain streaks diagonal lines across
    Main Street that glows neon in the storm.
White light circles each tree branch, sliding

sheets of memory. Life floats in simultaneous
    layers of the known and the unknown. Nowhere
is the reckless rhythm so indelibly scarred.

I rest my clouded hand on your cheek,
    secret child. Is this what you wanted me to see?
In the outer envelope, is there a muscle that

holds the two halves together. Restless questions
    drift into the invisible grid from forgotten places.
Planets spin outside the heart where we least

expect gardens. Morning sun rays through
    overgrown geraniums split the Persian rug into
patterns of light. Even with taproots twisted

bitter and deep, I have always loved
    you. Dandelions prop their sphered seed
heads up on hollow leafless stems,

then radiate—
wind spread

Ghosts Through Birds Calling

Pink claws extended, a cardinal flies up
    to the weeping cherry branch.
    Sun stripes shadows onto cobblestones.

The Solar System circles low near
    the horizon, as the Moon appears impossibly
    large. A baby mouse curls, a dark crescent

at the bottom of a bucket, her mouth
    frozen open as if this were the first death.
    Abandoning all illusion of safety, it is

today again. The point of my life shrinks
    like a tired star. A hair brush, a calendar,
    a spool of black thread, this is what

has been given. The faint organization
    of rings, murky river currents circle
    unruly. As far as the eye can see

above, even below ground, networks of dying
    trees link to feed young saplings. Beyond
    the wrought iron, a locked gate,

as wings thrum in the outer courtyard
    like ghosts through birds calling.
    Pale like the inside of a shell, an echo

of someone long gone whispers something
    I cannot understand. A door slams.
    Then silence. Where space bends

Beekeepers, Jugglers and Pilgrims

Friday the Town Assessor comes
    to inspect the attic. Water-stained roof
        boards pierced with nails, at the bottom

of a leak bucket, a petrified baby bat
    lies paper flaked. One week away
        from the half moon, earth crusts shift.

Lunar rhythms pull the tides, turning
    the universe backward on its axis. Earth mites
        crawl through cracks in the ground, their shark

like teeth. The galaxy spinning too
    fast, female mites lay eggs along the rim
        of our face pores, I keep watch in my sleep.

Does a distant god enjoy the rustle
    of our fear? In New Zealand's night,
        crickets freeze solid only to come alive

again in daylight warmth. A black-spotted
    oval-domed ladybug swirls in my tea water
        before boiling. With soup spoon, I scoop

her out, lay her on the rug where she waddles
    away. Beekeepers, jugglers and pilgrims, we
        want so many things. We dangle our illusions

from the thread of a high note. Gather all
    the loose items you can: tablespoons and bones,
        dried flesh, yarn and eggs. Dedicate yourself to a skill

before a crow's call can break the spell

Writing While Driving Across the Tappan Zee Bridge

A fog so dense, I drive ahead
enclosed in a separate world. A member
of the generation raised ignored and unseen, I
swallow each day like a fisherman afraid of the ocean.

The first thing I learned
in college after the in loco
parentis lecture on the necessity
of virginity, was how to roll a joint.
I paced corn fields reciting poems to
communities of stars, as night sky engulfed
the land. The first time I left you, I hitchhiked
into dawn, sawdust puppets tucked into a laundry
bag on one shoulder, a broken guitar on the other. Out
Route 68, I boomeranged back to suburban cocktail parties,
adults sipping scotch, their cells embedded with cigarette smoke.

> Across the Tappan Zee, where slabs of concrete had
> crashed into the river leaving openings in pavement
> large enough to see down into the Hudson, I examine
> my wrinkled face in the mirror. A ghost of myself ringed
> with colored mists, the clown in me gives me courage.

Some pray to the crescent
moon. Some thrash their wings
unable to fly. Lucky ones drive ahead as if
there was nothing to fear. Some scribble on paper
scraps on the steering wheel, to capture whatever they can.

We balance, one-legged
toppling unmetered through dreams
to risk the unknown before the absorption
of all palpable light. We sing and we sing, wanting
only to touch the moving silhouette before it disappears

Wild Phlox

I hike the curved alphabet of wild phlox. Light
reflected haze turns a blue circle over slabs of rock.

A squirrel chitters from the railing, the outline
of Solomon's seal in the most unexpected places.

Sweet words solid as wind, my tongue no longer
mine, I listen for seasons to change. I try to gather

enough echinacea to take back the years, the sadness
of flesh. Sunlight shudders over gravestones of those

who have gone before me. I yank out creeper vines
that twist through my porch railing. One eye open,

the other eye closed, my white hair falls like feathers.
Do you dream of floating in lavender mist, spinning

in silver shoes? I fear a structure so fragile, a breeze
could split it open. I cover my mouth with my hand.

To steady myself, I wrap my hope around the tip
of a cherry blossom bud just about to open—

breathe into the wound of a new poem

The Leather Jacket

Worn soft like the skin of earth,
metal zipper broken half off, I coax it up
the ladder of teeth to protect against needles of wind.

I slip keys into an unraveled pocket
that topples them into a canyon, a rift in
the sky, the dark universe of burned-down bones.

I thread the needle.
Not as sharp as the pain
of loss. Cotton the color of fawn.

Where pocket separates
from body, I pierce the tip. Push
the eye into the open mouth of cloth, pulling

two halves of the universe together again. I breathe
into the space between what is and what could be

Amaryllis

Marionettes rise black against the supermoon,
human silhouettes of what was once believed

to be true. If personality cracks first, then the soul,
is there even a name for the distance in spheres

this forgotten. We wait, uncertain in the last room
to be chosen, an unearthed map. Your shadow

skirts a truth woven from tired strands. Is this
what you wanted me to see? Through the storm,

lace beads freeze rain streaks into diagonals
that throb neon down Main Street. White light

surrounds each drop. Words slip away from my
sentences. I call on the ones who gave me words,

on the bodies of parents in cement graves, on
the small villages that run through my veins.

I call on the amaryllis bud, that just before
blossoming holds itself full to bursting

Nothing in the Silk Air

Nothing in the silk air today fits
this handful of planets. This blind

morning. If I could feel a solid step,
the opening or closing of a hand,

ribs that separate in prayer for breath.
A cardinal, dusty stomach puffed

out with too many holly berries from
the bush by the driveway, a web

of lines to separate from the burning
cord. You could say—just turn the key.

Shift the Celica into reverse. Back over
fallen chestnut hulls, accelerate

through the promise of mountain
mist. You could say, but isn't this

where time opens up. Isn't this
where you know yourself best

Remains of the Formal Garden

A white-tailed deer flicks her right ear,
bolts through remains of the formal

gardens. I curl into leaves by
the water, click the door closed.

Dust particles circle the afternoon
sun. A raven swoops low almost

touching light spheres on the lake.
Calm in the pale rain at the tip of

the hurricane's wing, a drop of blood
from one god, a tear from another.

Furless, featherless, scaleless, a voice
too little, if I could learn the names

of things, weave something perfect I may
never understand. I yearn for another self,

    the one not afraid to stand alone
    in a field of blossoming flowers

to come looking for me

The Glory

"A Glory is an optical phenomenon that resembles an iconic saint's halo about the shadow of the observer's head, caused by light of the Sun… interacting with the tiny water droplets that make up mist or clouds."

—*Wikipedia*

Position yourself barefoot in garlic mustard on a mountain top
where bittersweet's scarlet berries have held on long after its leaves
have gone. Look to the other side of the Sun. A lens of droplets
casts a shadow into the opposite side of the sky. Your ghost will loom

giant, a colored mist, a wingless phantom in early morning.
You do not have to borrow a happy childhood.
You do not have to open your skin.
If you pause there, watch from a roof above rough seas where

the world is pulled out of the map of itself. Breathe in a sequence
long enough for the horizon to spin as if you could gather up all
the years that have been lost and boulders of impossibility had begun
to melt. Before your edges fog across the clouds, before the rain erases

the mountain, before you feel the familiar half-life pull of someone
calling from far away, take off your winged helmet. Take off your silver
boots. Trace the long roots of dry land. Descend the mountain into
your heavy cloak of skin. Spread your fingers across the sky to measure

the distance to heaven as you feel the beating heart in each
thing. Place the pieces you gave away to be loved beside
the outline of half-remembered people.
Tame the wild doubt of your tiny heart.

You will not fall

The Fragmented Path

The unraveling of creeper vines
jaw bone link to skull snaps shut,
it is too late in the night for any
one to love me. Earth tilts toward
the Sun increasing the length of days.
The mountains flood with snowmelt
after warm rains. What if you could
split apart everything you once thought
belonged—the fragmented path,
arrangement of atoms, click into
the electric field as if everything
mattered? A robin picks at a clump
of holly berries. Dust grows into a star.
Can you hear them in the night, wind
shear above waves? The low speed
soaring, a rushing sweet enough
to blow apart the limb bone of an angel

Four Fierce Angels

A preference for gleaning tangled vines,
    I sometimes fear the smallest things.
    Forsythia still yellow, after the rains

azaleas not yet crimson, sprout small
    leaves. An opossum darts into a privet
    hedge. Planets look as if they're stopped

in the sky. Pigeons flutter in the hallway
    shaft toward dawn. Afterward there are
    errands. Things to buy, separating what

I can do from what I cannot do. Trapped
    between hope and sadness, as if I were part
    of the pattern too. If I could swell away

from this used skin, birth a new self. Here
    and there a crow or the sound of a passing
    car. A white butterfly hovers over the rose

bush. A humming bird dips into dream
    lush angel hollyhock flowers larger than
    the spread of my hand. For one moment

the world is completely balanced on its axis.
    Four fierce angels face left.
    I will try to love that much.

Anique Sara Taylor holds a Poetry MFA (Drew University), a Diplôme (The Sorbonne), a Painting BFA and Drawing MFA (Pratt Institute). Her work has appeared in *Rattle, Common Ground Review, Adanna, Stillwater Review, Earth's Daughters, The World* (St. Mark's Poetry Project), *The National Poetry Magazine of the Lower East Side* among others. Her chapbook *Poems* is published by Unimproved Editions Press. She's co-authored works for HBO, Scholastic, Simon & Schuster and a three-act play that was performed by Playwrights Horizons and Williamstown Theatre Festival.

Her work has appeared in several anthologies: *The Lake Rises* (Stockport Flats Press), *Pain and Memory* (Editions Bibliotekos, Inc.), *Veils, Halos and Shackles: International Poetry on the Oppression and Empowerment of Women* (Kasva Press).

An award-winning artist, Taylor's art has been featured in numerous galleries including The Bruce Museum, CT, The Monmouth Museum, NJ, The Noyes Museum, NJ, The Puffin Foundation, NJ, The Cork Gallery at Avery Fisher Hall, NYC, The Bronfman Center Gallery, NYC.

She teaches Creative Writing for Benedictine Hospital's Oncology Support Program, Bard LLI and Writers in the Mountains.

CPSIA information can be obtained
at www.ICGtesting.com
Printed in the USA
LVHW110609221220
674783LV00006B/928

9 781646 621866